W.B. YEATS

One of the greatest figures of twentieth-century writing, W.B. Yeats was awarded the Nobel Prize for Literature in 1927. His life was full of variety and his interests wide-ranging – from poetry to theatre, politics to spiritualism.
From Celtic legends and ancient sagas, as well as from his own experience, he created a world literature.

THE AUTHORS

Mary Moriarty lives in Dublin with her husband and three children. She took a degree with the Open University in arts and has taught in the Adult Literacy scheme in Dun Laoghaire.

Catherine Sweeney took a degree in arts at UCD, and has worked as a teacher at secondary level and as a translator and interpreter. She lives with her husband and children in Dublin.

MARY MORIARTY

CATHERINE SWEENEY

THE O'BRIEN PRESS
DUBLIN

First published 1988 by The O'Brien Press Ltd.,
20 Victoria Road, Rathgar, Dublin 6, Ireland
Copyright © text Mary Moriarty and Catherine Sweeney
Drawings © The O'Brien Press.

2   4   6   8   10   9   7   5   3
96   98   00   02   04   03   01   99   97   95

British Library Cataloguing-in-Publication Data
Moriarty, Mary
W.B. Yeats.
1.Poetry in English. Yeats, W.B. (William Butler), 1865-1939.
Biographies
I. Title II. Sweeney, Catherine
III. Rooney, David
821'.8
ISBN 0-86278-161-2

Typesetting, design, editing: The O'Brien Press
Book illustrations: David Rooney
Cover painting: Sean O'Sullivan
Courtesy of the Abbey Theatre
Cover design: Neasa Ní Chianáin
Cover separations: Lithoset
Printing: The Guernsey Press Ltd.

CONTENTS

*Yeats as a young man, painted
by his father.*

ACKNOWLEDGEMENTS

*The authors and publisher thank the following for permission
to reproduce photographs: Bord Failte pages 9, 24, 33, 39, 45,
57; National Gallery of Ireland 6, 11, 21, 41; National Library
of Ireland 12; Hugh Lane Gallery 29; RTE 50; Mary Moriarty
55; An Post 25.*

*Permission for extracts from The Collected Works of W.B. Yeats
courtesy A.P. Watt Ltd. on behalf of Michael B. Yeats and
Macmillan London Ltd.*

In 1863 when Susan Pollexfen, thought to be 'the most beautiful girl in Sligo', married John Butler-Yeats, a handsome young barrister, and settled into their new home at 5 Sandymount Avenue in Dublin, she must have looked forward to a long and enjoyable life among the best Dublin society. Susan was the daughter of William Pollexfen, a wealthy shipowner in Sligo. John's uncle, Robert Corbet, lived just a short walk away at Sandymount Castle, then a lovely house with large well-kept gardens and deer roaming the park. The young couple often visited the castle, and Robert Corbet, who was very hospitable, was delighted to have his nephew and his wife living nearby.

John and Susan's first son was born on 13 June 1865 at their house in Sandymount. They named him William Butler after his grandfather, who was a Church of Ireland curate in County Down. Another ancestor, John Yeats, had been rector of Drumcliff in County Sligo in 1805. The Yeats family connection with Sligo can be traced back to this clergyman.

For the first few years after his marriage John Butler Yeats practised as a barrister at the Law

Courts in Dublin, but he was more interested in drawing and sketching the heads and faces he saw about him in the courts than in the practice of the law. After a while he decided to give up his legal career and become a full-time artist. First he would go and study at an art college in London.

This news must have come as quite a shock to poor Susan who had absolutely no interest in painting or art. Throughout their married life she never once went to John's studio to see him work or even to an exhibition of paintings. He did, however, paint her portrait.

LONDON

In 1868 the Yeats family moved to 23 Fitzroy Road, Regent's Park, London, and this was to be their home for the next six years. Susan missed Ireland, the Pollexfen family and, above all, Sligo. She loved her native Sligo with its bay, its trading ships and fishing boats. She loved to hear the stories of the local fishing people and she told these tales of seafaring adventures, ghosts and fairies to her children. She told them too of her own childhood in Sligo and of the beauty of the county and in this way she passed her great love of the place and its folklore on to her children. As William said later, 'It was always assumed between her and us that Sligo was more beautiful than other places.'

There were five Yeats children. William was the eldest and would grow up to be a great poet. Jack, the second boy, became a painter like his father. For much of his early life Jack painted Irish country people and rural scenes. He loved to paint tinkers, the circus coming to town, a fair day or races on the strand. Up to this time only important people and

Ben Bulben in Sligo. When Yeats was a child he considered Sligo the most beautiful place on earth.

romantic landscapes had been painted. Nobody had ever bothered to paint ordinary Irish people enjoying themselves.

Robert, the third son, died as a child and William remembers a servant in the house telling his mother that the night before Robert died she heard the *Beansi* wailing for him. There was a belief among country people in Ireland that if the *Beansi* was heard wailing in the night someone in the house would die shortly afterwards. There were two girls, Susan, who was called Lilly by the family, and

Elizabeth, who was known as Lolly. After many years in London the two sisters returned to Dublin and set up the Cuala Press, with which William also became involved. The press was famous for its production of beautiful books of poetry and ballads.

VISITS TO SLIGO

Though the Yeats family were living in London, Susan and the children made long visits to Merville, her family home in Sligo. They were able to travel home from England to Sligo on one of their grandfather Pollexfen's boats. At Merville young Willie had a little red pony to ride and two dogs who followed him around everywhere he went. The house was big and spacious with lots of places for a small boy to hide in if he wanted to be alone.

William was a very shy and sensitive young boy and when he was ticked off by a grandparent or aunt he would often 'have a night of misery' worrying about his sins. In later life, when writing about his boyhood, he said, 'I remember little of childhood but its pain.' Why this was so he could not remember, as everyone was kind to him.

William was very slow to learn to read. Several of his aunts and uncles tried to teach him and failed and they began to think he was stupid as he was much older than children who could read easily. This state of affairs might have gone on much longer but for the arrival of his father on a visit to Sligo.

John Yeats never went to church and though William loved God and tried his best to please him, he hated going to church because his grandmother was always telling him on the way there to walk properly. So one Sunday, when he saw his father was not joining the family at church, he too refused

John Butler Yeats, William's father — a self portrait.

Yeats at ten years of age.

to go. There and then, his father decided to teach
him to read. John Yeats turned out to be a very
cross and impatient teacher and when young
William was slow to learn he flung the book at the
boy's head. This was too much for Willie, and the
following Sunday he was back at church with the

rest of the family. However, his father, who was now determined that his son would learn to read, changed the lessons to the middle of the week. Once he knew there was no way out, William put his mind to the work and shortly afterwards succeeded.

GODOLPHIN SCHOOL

The family moved to West Kensington in 1874 and the following year William was sent to his first proper school, the Godolphin School in Hammersmith. For a young boy of ten who had never been to a big school the Godolphin seemed very rough. Older boys punched younger ones just to see them double up in pain. William hated this bullying and being thin, gaunt and Irish he was often taunted and given many a black eye.

He decided that the best way to deal with the situation was to be, or at least to pretend to be, tougher than the others. So, although he was terrified of plunging into the swimming baths, he steeled himself to dive from great heights. His best friend at school was a boy who was a good athlete. He often fought William's battles for him and he even brought him home to teach him to box so that he could defend himself properly. Yeats told how, in battles with the street boys near their school, he always ran with the others but never hit anyone. In class he often sat dreaming and 'instead of learning my lessons I covered the white squares of the chess-board on my little table with pen and ink pictures of myself doing all kinds of courageous things.'

While William was at Godolphin School the family moved again, this time to Bedford Park, a new garden suburb and a much more pleasant place to live. The visits to Sligo became less frequent, probably because of a shortage of money, though the Yeats children still pined for their mother's home. In his autobiography William describes sitting with his sister by the drinking fountain near Holland Park and being near to tears as they spoke of their longing for Sligo and their hatred of London and how he yearned for a 'sod of earth from some field I knew, something from Sligo to hold in my hand.'

RETURN TO DUBLIN

Four years later, in 1880, the Yeats family was on the move again. This time, to William and his mother's delight, it was back to Ireland. William was now fifteen years old. They rented a thatched cottage on the cliff-top above the busy fishing village of Howth. The cottage must have been very exposed, for on windy nights the spray would lash the house. William, who had developed a passion for the open air and had removed his entire window, often woke to find his bed soaked. He sometimes left the house at night to sleep in a nearby cave and he would take with him a candle, a tin of cocoa and some biscuits for a snack. On fine nights he slept under the rhododendrons in the grounds of Howth Castle.

A year later the family left the cottage and moved to a house overlooking the harbour at Howth. This move pleased Susan Yeats most of all. The coming and going of the fishing fleet and the busy life around the harbour must have reminded Susan of her beloved Sligo. William's happiest memories of his mother are of seeing her swopping stories over a cup of tea in their kitchen with a fisherman's wife who was a servant in the house, both women laughing and enjoying the tales. Later he would use many

William sometimes spent the night in a cave.

of those stories in the poem 'Village Ghosts' in *Celtic Twilight*, the first book he had published.

John Yeats, who now earned his living as a painter, had taken a studio in York Street, near St Stephen's Green, in the centre of Dublin. He enrolled William at the Erasmus Smith High School which was just around the corner in Harcourt Street. High School, as it is known in Dublin, still exists but is now situated in Rathgar. Every morning William and his father would take the train from Howth into Dublin and have breakfast together at the studio. During breakfast John would read poetry or passages from famous plays to his son. Father and son would discuss what had been read and then William would go off to school while his father spent the day painting. In the evening they would return to Howth by train.

During this period John Butler Yeats was a great influence on his son. He believed there was more to education than the set subjects at school. He wanted to develop the boy's imagination and to broaden his knowledge. He knew William had some special talent and he was determined that he would not be tied to schoolbooks. He wanted him to be free to explore all the great works of literature and art. He discussed the works of Keats, Shelley, Wordsworth and Shakespeare with him. He introduced him to the great works of art, pointing out the artists' different styles and techniques. He encouraged his son to think about these artists and writers and to form his own opinions about them. Above all he encouraged the boy to use his own imagination freely and without restraint. It was about this time

Breakfast at John Yeats's studio.

that William began to write poetry. By the time he left High School, where he had been a mediocre student, he could not decide whether he wanted to be a painter or a writer.

THE COLLEGE OF ART

At the age of eighteen Yeats entered the College of Art in Kildare Street. One of his closest friends there was another student, George Russell, who called himself AE. Like Yeats, AE was interested in magic, in visions and in the invisible world of spirits and fairies. They would often go up the Dublin mountains to places like Kilmashogue where it is said the old Celtic gods are buried, hoping to see visions and communicate with the spirit world.

A BUDDING POET

In 1884 Yeats left the College of Art and decided to make writing his fulltime career. At this time the family moved from Howth to Harold's Cross. His mother was very sad to leave the seaside village. She missed the long chats with the fisherman's wife about fishing people and tales of the sea. The family was now quite poor, as Yeats's father was still not making much money from his painting.

By this time Yeats had been writing poetry for several years and in 1885 his poetry appeared in print for the first time. Yeats now began to get involved in the life of Dublin city. The 1880s were a time of intense debate on many topics. There was a lot of discussion about Charles Stewart Parnell, the leader of the Irish Party, and his campaign for Home Rule. Ireland at this time was governed by the British parliament in London. The Home Rule movement wanted a parliament in Dublin to look after local Irish affairs while the parliament in London would continue to look after the larger international issues, such as peace and war.

The Fenians were another group active in Ireland at the time. They wanted complete independence for Ireland with the London parliament having no say whatever in the government of Ireland.

A third major movement of the time was the Land League, founded by Michael Davitt. In the 1880s it was only forty years since the disastrous famine in Ireland. There were many people still alive who had suffered great hardship and had been evicted from their homes by the landlords during this famine. The Land League wanted ownership of the land to be transferred to the tenant farmers so that the people would no longer be at the mercy of the landlords.

IRISH HISTORY AND POLITICS

Yeats went with his father to many meetings where these issues were discussed and he developed an interest in the history and politics of Ireland. These meetings were also important to Yeats as they gave him an opportunity to practise speaking in public. He was rather shy but he wanted to be able to speak calmly and confidently in front of an audience, so he always got involved in the discussions at the meetings. Sometimes, in the heat of an argument, he would get confused and be unable to express himself very well. He tells us in his autobiography that on these occasions 'I would spend hours afterwards going over my words and putting the wrong ones right'.

He met many important people at these meetings but the most important person for him was a man called John O'Leary. O'Leary was an old Fenian who had been imprisoned and exiled for his activities in the Fenian movement. Yeats met him in 1885 when he had returned to Ireland from exile. He wrote later, 'From O'Leary's conversation and from the Irish books he lent or gave me has come all I have set my hand to since.' O'Leary's love for Ireland had a lasting effect on Yeats. He used to call regularly to O'Leary's house where he met other young people and spent long hours in talk and discussion. There he met a young poet, Katherine Tynan, who later described him as 'all dreams and gentleness, beautiful to look at with his dark face, its touch of vivid colouring, the night black hair, the eager dark eyes ... he lived, breathed, ate, drank and slept poetry.'

All these experiences opened up to Yeats a part of Ireland he had been almost unaware of. Yeats was a Protestant and his family were Anglo-Irish. The Anglo-Irish were descended from English settlers in Ireland. In those days, when Ireland was part of the British Empire, the ruling class in Dublin was Protestant. Protestants owned the banks and all the big industries and filled all the important positions in the civil service. They rarely mixed socially with the Catholic population and would, to a large extent, have been unaware of the fact that there was a native Irish culture stretching back for hundreds of years. Therefore, for Yeats, a Protestant, it was exciting to be in O'Leary's house where Catholic and Protestant young people mixed and discussed the history and literature of Ireland and where people were aware of such things as the ancient Irish legends of Fionn MacCumhaill and the Red Branch Knights.

John O'Leary, painted by William's father.

Up to now nearly all the literature that had been written by Irish people in English had very little to do with Irish culture or traditions. Yeats resolved that it was now time for Ireland to have a distinct literature of her own in English. He wanted his own poetry to be recognisably Irish.

When we read his poetry we can see how well he succeeded. His poems are full of Ireland, of the Sligo countryside he loved so much, of the fairy stories he had heard from the country people and of the old Irish legends. In 'The Stolen Child' he tells us of the fairies playing in the waters of Glencar Waterfall and dancing by moonlight on the sands at Rosses Point. These are places he knew well from his visits to Sligo. The poem tells of a human child being lured away from human suffering to a magic fairyland. Here are verses three and four:

Where the wandering water gushes
From the hills above Glen-Car
In pools among the rushes
That scarce could bathe a star,
We seek for slumbering trout
And whispering in their ears
Give them unquiet dreams;
leaning softly out
From ferns that drop their tears
Over the young streams.
Come away, O human child!
To the waters and the wild
With a faery, hand in hand,
For the world's more full of weeping
    than you can understand.

Away with us he's going,
The solemn-eyed:
He'll hear no more the lowing
Of the calves on the warm hillside
Or the kettle on the hob
Sing peace into his breast,
Or see the brown mice bob
Round and round the oatmeal-chest.
For he comes, the human child,
To the waters and the wild
With a faery, hand in hand,
From a world more full of weeping
    than he can understand.

As his friend Katherine Tynan said, Yeats lived
and breathed poetry. He used to keep his sisters
awake at night sitting downstairs by the fire recit-
ing poetry out loud. His mind was so full of poetry
and imaginings that he was often very absent-
minded. One time Katherine gave him some pills to
take when he wasn't feeling well and he absent-min-
dedly took them all at the same time, after which
he slept for thirty hours!

Yeats's father didn't prosper as a portrait painter
in Ireland, so in 1887 the family moved back to London, to Bedford Park. There were many artists, writers and actors living around them here and William
met many of the important writers of the time, including Oscar Wilde, Robert Louis Stevenson, Ru-
dyard Kipling and George Bernard Shaw.

He was very busy writing and early in 1889, with
money organised for him by John O'Leary and other
friends, he published his first book of poetry. It was
called *Wanderings of Oisin and Other Poems*. The

Glencar Waterfall in Sligo.

Commemorative stamps celebrating Yeats and some of his contemporaries: George Bernard Shaw, J.M. Synge, Oscar Wilde, Jack B. Yeats

main poem in this collection is based on an old Irish legend. It tells the story of the wanderings of Oisin, Fionn MacCumhail's son, with his fairy lover, Niamh. Yeats was delighted when it was praised by the critics.

MAUD GONNE

Not long after the publication of this book, there arrived at the door of the house in Bedford Park a person who was to have the most profound effect on Yeats's life and poetry. This person was Maud Gonne. She was tall, had red-gold hair and golden eyes and was so strikingly beautiful that Yeats fell in love with her at first sight. Yeats later described her as he saw her that day: 'Her complexion was luminous, like that of apple-blossom through which light falls and I remember her standing that first day by a great heap of such blossoms in the window.' When he met her she was twenty-two and he was twenty-three. Yeats was to remain passionately in love with her for almost the next thirty years and he would write many beautiful love poems to her. Here is one of them:

He Wishes for the Cloths of Heaven

Had I the heavens' embroidered cloths,
Enwrought with golden and silver light,
The blue and the dim and the dark cloths
Of night and light and the half-light,
I would spread the cloths under your feet:
But I, being poor, have only my dreams;
I have spread my dreams under your feet;
Tread softly because you tread on my dreams.

He wishes for the cloths of heaven

Had I the heavens' embroidered cloths,
Enwrought with golden and silver light,
The blue and the dim and the dark cloths
Of night and light and half-light;
I would spread the cloths under your feet;
But I, being poor, have only my dreams;
I have spread my dreams under your feet,
Tread softly because you tread on my dreams.

Maud Gonne, however, did not return his love. They remained friends for many years and for a long time Yeats never gave up hope of winning her heart. Although she was English and the daughter of a colonel in the British army, she hated the fact that Ireland was ruled by England. She was involved in many movements and groups that were trying to overthrow British rule in Ireland. She did a lot of work in the rural areas of Ireland helping poor people who had been evicted from their homes and setting up soup kitchens to give them food. The combination of her great beauty and her compassion for the poor had such an effect on people that wherever she went in Ireland large crowds gathered to see her pass and people would reach out to touch the hem of her coat.

Maud Gonne travelled a lot and for years after their first meeting she would meet Yeats whenever she was in London. In his autobiography he wrote: 'In the next few years I saw her always when she passed to and fro between Dublin and Paris, surrounded, no matter how rapid her journey and how brief her stay at either end of it, by cages full of birds, canaries, finches of all kinds, dogs, a parrot and once a full grown hawk from Donegal.'

To distract himself from his unhappy love for Maud Gonne, Yeats plunged into a ceaseless round of activities. He was still interested in magic and in 1890 he joined a group called The Order of the Golden Dawn. This group tried to build up an understanding of the life of the spirit and the soul by practising and studying a mixture of magic and beliefs taken from Christianity and eastern religions.

In 1891 Yeats helped set up a group of poets

A painting by Sarah Purser of Maud Gonne,
whom Yeats loved for many years.

called 'The Rhymers' Club'. He wrote to a friend explaining why he wanted such a club: 'I am growing jealous of other poets and we will all grow jealous of each other unless we know each other and feel a share in each other's triumphs.' The poets listened to each other's poetry and discussed it. In the same year he founded the Irish Literary Society in London and in 1892 founded an Irish Literary Society in Dublin.

Yeats spent his days writing. He wrote poetry and plays and books of Irish fairy stories and legends. His love for Maud Gonne inspired him to write very beautiful love poems. Also, one of the plays he wrote at this time was *The Countess Cathleen* in which the heroine was also based on Maud. The play tells the story of a beautiful countess who sells her soul to the devil so that her people may be saved from starvation. God however, saves her from the devil and she is allowed into Heaven.

All this time Maud Gonne was still involved in her revolutionary activities. Yeats often visited Dublin and went to meetings and demonstrations with her.

In 1891 they attended the funeral of the Irish leader, Parnell. Yeats was very upset by the death of Parnell as he had had great respect for him. He realised that for a time Parnell had succeeded in uniting the two strands of Irish life — the Anglo-Irish and the Gaelic-Irish. Yeats dreamed of being able to do the same thing in Irish literature. He hoped to unite the Anglo-Irish and Gaelic-Irish traditions in a national literature.

He asked Maud Gonne to marry him several times. She turned him down but asked him to remain her friend. He continued to worship her and to write poetry about her and his love for her.

When You Are Old

When you are old and grey and full of sleep,
And nodding by the fire, take down this book,
And slowly read, and dream of the soft look
Your eyes had once, and of their shadows deep;

How many loved your moments of glad grace,
And loved your beauty with love false or true,
But one man loved the pilgrim soul in you,
And loved the sorrows of your changing face;
And bending down beside the glowing bars,
Murmur, a little sadly, how Love fled
And paced upon the mountains overhead
And hid his face amid a crowd of stars.

Yeats had many friends in London and his life was full of activity, but he hated living in the city and missed the beauty and tranquillity of the Sligo countryside. He describes the effect the city had on him in his autobiography: 'I grew oppressed by the great weight of stone and thought there are miles and miles of stone and brick all round me.' One day when he was walking through the city feeling homesick for Sligo he heard the noise of water falling from a fountain in a shop window. This reminded him of the sound of the water in Lough Gill near his grandfather's house.

Going home with his imagination full of memories of the lake and its islands, he wrote:

The Lake Isle of Innisfree

I will arise and go now, and go to Innisfree,
And a small cabin build there, of clay and wattles made:
Nine bean-rows will I have there, a hive for the
    honeybee,
And live alone in the bee-loud glade.

And I shall have some peace there, for peace comes dropping slow,
Dropping from the veils of the morning to where the cricket sings;
There midnight's all a glimmer, and noon a purple glow,
And evening full of the linnet's wings.

I will arise and go now, for always night and day
I hear lake water lapping with low sounds by the
    shore;
While I stand on the roadway, or on the pavements grey,
I hear it in the deep heart's core.

Although his home was in London, Yeats visited Ireland regularly. In 1894 he was invited to visit the Gore-Booth sisters in Sligo. They lived in Lissadell, a great mansion near Sligo town. The sisters were Eva Gore-Booth, a poet, and her sister Constance, better known as Countess Markievicz, who was

The Lake Isle of Innisfree in Sligo. Yeats often longed for the peace and tranquillity of the Sligo countryside.

later to take an active part in the 1916 Rising. Yeats enjoyed his visit to the house and celebrated it with the beautiful lines:

> The light of evening, Lissadell,
> Great windows open to the south,
> Two girls in silk kimonos, both
> beautiful, one a gazelle.

In 1895 Yeats moved into rooms in 18 Woburn Buildings. This was to be his London home for the next twenty-four years, until 1919. His home soon became a gathering place for London writers and artists. Every Monday evening they would meet in Yeats's rooms for conversation, poetry readings and discussions. He was now thirty years of age and was recognised as an important poet.

LADY GREGORY

In 1896, while on a visit to Galway, Yeats met Lady Augusta Gregory. He was later to say of her, 'I doubt if I should have done much with my life but for her firmness and care.' They took an immediate liking to each other and became firm friends. Lady Gregory lived in a beautiful old mansion called Coole Park. It was approached by a long tree-lined drive and was surrounded by woods behind which lay a lake where many swans built their nests. There is a lovely description of this lake in the poem 'The Wild Swans at Coole'.

Lady Gregory invited Yeats to stay at Coole Park and he gladly accepted. It was an ideal place for a poet to think and write, and the peace and tranquillity were particularly welcome to Yeats at this time as he was still suffering from his hopeless love for Maud Gonne.

Lady Gregory shared Yeats's interest in literature and in Irish culture and tradition. As a child she had been looked after by a Catholic nurse who had been employed years earlier in the household of Hamilton Rowan, a friend of Wolfe Tone and a prominent figure in the 1798 rebellion. From this nurse she heard tales of 1798 and old Irish stories and legends and this gave her a love of the ancient heritage of Ireland.

Yeats and Lady Gregory at Coole Park.

When they met the following year Yeats told Lady Gregory of his idea for an Irish theatre company. He hoped to set up a theatre company to present plays inspired by the old legends and folktales of Ireland, and reflecting its age-old culture. It was part of a plan he had had for a long time of creating a national literature. By presenting it on stage he hoped to reach a wider audience than could be reached by poetry alone.

This idea of a theatre that would present plays of an Irish character was something completely new. Plays based on Irish culture had never been written or presented on stage before. Lady Gregory was delighted with the idea. She was a great organiser and immediately worked out a plan to raise enough money to hire a theatre in Dublin to put Yeats's plan into action. They decided that the first play to be presented should be *The Countess Cathleen.*

Yeats spent most of the summer of 1897 at Coole Park and it soon became his second home. For the next thirteen years he spent every summer there and visited it at other times of the year also. The quiet ordered routine of the house appealed to him. He wrote, 'This house has enriched my soul out of measure because here life moves within restraint through gracious forms.'

Lady Gregory was very hospitable and there was a constant stream of guests at Coole Park. The guests were usually writers, artists and scholars so there was never a shortage of interesting and stimulating conversation. Among the people who stayed in the house at this time were Yeats's friends A.E.,

A seance. Yeats was fascinated by magic and the occult.

Douglas Hyde (who in 1893 had founded a society called the Gaelic League to preserve the Irish language, music and culture) and John Millington Synge, a playwright who was later to write some of the best plays for the new Irish theatre.

The old house at Coole is now no longer there but the 'autograph tree' can still be seen where Lady Gregory's guests, including Yeats, cut their initials.

Meanwhile, Yeats continued with his revolutionary activities directed against British rule in Ireland. In 1898 he was elected president of an international committee which had been set up to commemorate the rebellion against English rule which had taken place a hundred years earlier in 1798 in which Theobald Wolfe Tone played an important part. He organised and attended many meetings throughout Ireland and England. A final rally was held in St Stephen's Green to honour Wolfe Tone. An immense crowd gathered for this meeting. Yeats was one of the principal speakers and he was seated in a place of honour alongside Maud Gonne and his old friend, John O'Leary.

Yeats showed his disrespect for British rule in Ireland in other smaller ways also. For instance he rolled up the red carpets that had been spread to welcome important visiting members of the British Government!

The year 1899 was to prove extremely eventful for Yeats. At the beginning of the year his third book of poetry, *The Wind among the Reeds*, was published and work was underway on his Irish theatre.

After a lot of organisation and preparation the date was finally set for the first performance of the Irish Theatre. Two plays, Yeats's *The Countess Cathleen* and Edward Martyn's *The Heather Field*,

The autograph tree, where Lady Gregory's guests cut their initials. This picture shows the initials WBY (Yeats), SO'C (Seán O'Casey), GBS (George Bernard Shaw), among others.

were to be presented on 8 May 1899 in a small concert hall in Molesworth Street, Dublin.

THE COUNTESS CATHLEEN

Shortly before the first night, however, rumours began to spread around Dublin that the theme of *The Countess Cathleen* was not suitable for Catholic audiences. An enemy of Yeats wrote a pamphlet attacking the play, and the Irish cardinal of the time, Cardinal Logue, who had read the pamphlet but not the play itself, wrote a letter to a newspaper saying Catholics should not attend it. Many of Yeats's Catholic friends now refused to support the new Irish Theatre and students at University College Dublin issued a document condemning the play. One student who refused to sign this document was a young man called James Joyce, who was later to become one of the most famous writers of the twentieth century. At this time he was seventeen years of age.

Despite all this opposition the play opened on the date arranged. The hall was packed for the opening night and the play got a very noisy reception. There were a lot of people in the audience — mainly students — who were opposed to the play and who greeted the performance with boos and jeers. But they were shouted down by the rest of the audience who loved the play. The same thing happened every other evening, but the objectors were always outnumbered by those who were enthusiastic about seeing an Irish play on the stage. Yeats was delighted with the enthusiasm of the audience and he realised now that his idea of a national Irish theatre could become a reality.

Several nights after opening night a celebration banquet was held in the Shelbourne Hotel. Some of Yeats's closest friends were there — John O'Leary, AE, Douglas Hyde and many more. And so, in spite of all the objections, a successful beginning had been made towards providing Ireland with a theatre of her own. This would eventually lead to the establishment of the Abbey Theatre.

The next year, 1900, the Irish Theatre presented two further plays. This time they hired the Gaiety Theatre. Although this theatre was twice the size of the concert hall in Molesworth Street, used the year before, it was almost full every evening. Yeats and Lady Gregory were well pleased.

Maud Gonne as The Countess Cathleen.

Maud Gonne was very interested in the idea of an Irish theatre based on Irish culture and traditions and in 1902 she took the leading role in a new play by Yeats called *Cathleen Ní Houlihán*. The same year she became one of the vice-presidents of Yeats's Irish National Theatre. AE and Douglas Hyde were the other vice-presidents and Yeats was president.

These were exciting years for writers living in Dublin. The realisation that Ireland possessed a rich tradition in literature and folklore had caused great excitement among young writers and had led to an outpouring of talent. Among the famous writers living in Dublin at that time were Yeats, J.M. Synge, Pádraic Colum and James Stephens.

Before this, Dublin had been a backwater and if writers wanted to be recognised they had to go to London. Oscar Wilde and George Bernard Shaw, both born in Dublin, had gone to London thirty years earlier for this reason. We can see the change that had come about when we read Shaw's explanation for basing his work in London. He says that when he started writing: 'there was no Gaelic League then nor sense that Ireland had in herself the seed of culture. London was the literary centre for English literature and as the English language was my weapon, there was nothing for it but London.' What a change had been brought about by Yeats, Hyde and their friends. Dublin was now one of the leading centres of literary activity in Europe.

The year 1903 was both sad and very successful for Yeats. One evening in February, just before he was going to talk at a public meeting in Dublin, he was handed a letter from his beloved Maud Gonne. In the letter she told him that she had been married in Paris to Major John MacBride. Yeats was terribly upset by the news but he went on with the lecture. Afterwards he told friends that he had been so distressed he could not remember a single word he had said. He had loved Maud Gonne dearly from the moment he first saw her and while she remained single he had kept his hopes of marrying her alive. Later he wrote of his heartbreak:

But dear, cling close to me, since you were gone
My barren thoughts have chilled me to the bone.

Shortly afterwards he went on a lecture tour to the United States. The Americans loved Yeats. John Quinn, his close American friend, wrote to Lady Gregory that he was the greatest success in the States since Charles Stewart Parnell. The money he made from his lectures was a great help and would allow him to live comfortably. For the first time in his life he was free to write without any financial worries. The trip also kept him busy and helped him get over Maud's marriage.

Further success followed with the publication of three new books. These included a new book of poems, *In the Seven Woods*, and a book of essays. Yeats, who wanted to be a great writer and poet, was beginning to achieve his goal.

THE ABBEY THEATRE

Much to his delight the Irish National Theatre was making progress too. After a long search the Theatre found a permanent home in Abbey Street. This was partly due to the generosity of an English woman, Annie Horniman, a friend of Yeats who was very interested in the Theatre. When she heard what he and his friends were trying to do she gave them a large donation. With the move to Abbey Street the Theatre became known as the Abbey Theatre and it is still thriving today. In the early days all the actors and actresses came from England but later the Fay brothers, Frank and William, became involved and they trained Irish players. Many turned out to be very talented and became famous when the Abbey Players performed in London and New York.

There were difficulties at the Abbey. Some plays did not please the Irish public. Many people thought that the native Irish were being mocked by these new Anglo-Irish writers. During a performance of Synge's play, *The Playboy of the Western World*, which took place at the Abbey in January 1907, riots broke out in the theatre. The police had to be called to keep order and arrest the trouble-makers. The cast, though frightened, continued the play throughout the uproar. Lady Gregory telegraphed Yeats, who was in Scotland at the time, and he rushed back to Dublin. The riots caused great excitement in Dublin and students from Trinity and University College flocked to the Abbey to join in the fray. Yeats, who had by now overcome his shyness, loved a good row. He marched out on the stage and defended the play. A fierce argument took place between himself and the audience. He harangued everyone and won the day, refusing to take the play off. For the rest of its run the police stood guard in the theatre to prevent further trouble. Nowadays the play is regarded as a masterpiece.

Later that year Yeats visited Italy and toured some of the famous Renaissance cities, travelling

The Old Abbey Theatre in Dublin. It was destroyed by fire in 1951 and a new theatre was built in 1966, still called the Abbey Theatre.

to Florence, Ferrara and Urbino. He was very impressed by these beautiful places and recalled them later in his poetry. Yeats loved Italy and was to return there in his old age to spend the winter months at Rapallo, where he found great peace away from the 'bitterness of Irish quarrels'.

In 1909 his *Collected Works in Verse and Prose* was published. The following year, in recognition of his talent, he was invited to join the Royal Society of Literature. He was also given a pension by the British government which he accepted on condition that he could continue to write on Irish political issues. Many nationalists attacked him for accepting this pension.

YEATS'S VISION OF A NEW IRELAND

The early 1900s were stormy years in Ireland, particularly in Dublin. The country was buzzing with political activity. The spirit of nationalism was spreading among the people. A land reform movement was demanding action. James Connolly had founded the Socialist Party and Jim Larkin had come to Dublin from Belfast to organise a trade union among the dock and mill workers. The issue of Home Rule was smouldering in the background. The Unionists were organising against it and the nationalist community was organising in support of it. Yeats viewed the turmoil from London and did not like what he saw. He was saddened by the turn of events.

Yeats, who had a vision of a new Ireland where the native Irish people would develop their own political and cultural identity, did not like the petty and narrow path the people were taking. In the

*Yeats argues with the crowd during
the riots caused by the performance of
'The Playboy of the Western World'.*

poem 'September 1913' he questions what is happening to his fellow countrymen in the famous lines:

Romantic Ireland's dead and gone,
It's with O'Leary in the grave.

The poem was an appeal to the people to snap out of their narrow ways and to be more noble in their outlook like the gallant Irish of the past. Little did Yeats think that just three years later, following the 1916 Rebellion, he would again be writing to the people but this time on a very different theme. He composed 'Easter 1916' a few weeks after the leaders of the rising had been executed. Maud Gonne's husband, Major MacBride, was one of those executed. The poem commemorates the rebels' heroic deeds:

I write it out in a verse —
MacDonagh and MacBride
And Connolly and Pearse
Now and in time to be,
Wherever green is worn,
Are changed, changed utterly:
A terrible beauty is born.

And Yeats was so right. Many in Ireland were against the Rising of 1916 and were glad when the leaders surrendered and the violence stopped. However, when the English executed these men, in twos and threes over a period of days, the Irish were shocked and horrified and the mood of the country changed and swung right behind the rebels.

Yeats, who was still living in London, visited Dublin to see the ruined city. He was deeply affected

Yeats in Italy.

O'Connell Street devastated by the fighting in 1916.

by what he saw. He wondered too whether anything he had written earlier had helped drive the leaders to rebellion and their death.

Did that play of mine send out
Certain men the English shot?

He was distressed to find another old friend, the Countess Markievicz, in jail under sentence of death for her part in the rising. She was Constance Gore-Booth from Lissadell in Sligo, and had become Countess Markievicz on marriage. Yeats remembers her in happier times riding 'under Ben Bulben to the meet' in the poem 'On a Political Prisoner'.

Her death sentence was cancelled and later she became the first woman ever elected to the House of Parliament in England.

THOOR BALLYLEE AND MARRIAGE

Later in that eventful year Yeats returned to Ireland, this time to buy a place of his own in the west. He found exactly what he wanted at Ballylee, near Gort. It was perfectly situated just a few miles from Lady Gregory's home. It was an old tower with a little cottage attached to it and although it was in terrible condition Yeats loved the idea of living and writing in a tower. He immediately made plans to have it re-roofed and renovated as a summer home.

In 1917 he set off to visit Maud Gonne in France. As she was now a widow and free to marry again he proposed to her. Yet again she refused his offer. He later proposed to her daughter Iseult but she too refused him. Yeats seems to have been quite determined to find a wife, for in the autumn of the same year he married George Hyde-Lees, an English woman he had known for some years. The poet Ezra Pound was best man at the wedding.

George proved to be just the right wife for Yeats who was now fifty-two years of age. She, like the poet, was very interested in the spirit world and the mystical side of life. Shortly after their marriage Yeats discovered that his wife had a special capacity for 'automatic writing'. This was a system of writing which seemed to happen by itself when a person sat down with paper and pen and went into a trance-like state. Yeats, who had for many years tried out this system without much success, was thrilled with his wife's gift. It was to be a bond between them for the rest of their lives.

After a year in England Yeats brought George to live in Dublin. He had hoped to spend the summer at his tower near Gort but it was still not repaired. He was also very anxious to take his wife to Coole Park but the visit had to be postponed because of the tragic death of Lady Gregory's only son Robert. He had been shot down over Italy during the First World War and Lady Gregory was grief-stricken. Yeats wrote a poem mourning the young airman. In May he took George to Coole and much to his delight Lady Gregory and his wife liked each other at once. The Yeats couple stayed nearby for the summer months.

While in the west of Ireland, George helped supervise the repairs on the tower, which Yeats had called Thoor Ballylee. The poet was really excited about going to live in his new home and he dedicated the tower to his wife in a lovely poem which is inscribed on a stone there:

I, the poet William Yeats
With old millboards and sea-green slates
And smithy work from the Gort forge,
Restored this tower for my wife George.
And may these characters remain,
When all is ruin once again.

The last two lines were to come true and the tower which was neglected after the poet's death became a ruin again. Happily, thanks largely to the efforts of the Kiltartan Society, founded by Mary Hanley of Limerick, and Bord Fáilte, the tower has once again been restored.

Yeats and his wife returned to Dublin for the winter months and in the spring of 1919 their first child, Anne, was born. Much to the family's delight they were able to move into Thoor Ballylee that summer. He wrote to his American friend John Quinn that the tower had become his 'monument and symbol', and in a letter to his father said: 'I am writing in the great ground floor of the castle — pleasantest room I have yet seen.' There was still much work to be done but Yeats loved the house, and the poems which were published in a volume entitled *The Tower* were inspired by the place. It was indeed 'a place full of history and romance'. He was to spend many happy summers at Thoor Ballylee with George, Anne and a son Michael, who was born in 1921.

George found a large house at 82 Merrion Square in Dublin where they would spend winters. They moved to Merrion Square in September 1922.

INDEPENDENCE

By this time the war with the British was over and Ireland had become an independent country. A treaty had been signed between the British and the Irish, setting up a Free State of twenty-six counties of Ireland, while the six northern counties remained under British rule. An Irish government was then set up in Dublin with two chambers of parliament, the Dáil and the Senate. Many of the people who had fought in the war against the British were not satisfied with the division of Ireland that had been agreed in the treaty. A civil war broke out between those who supported the new Irish government and those who opposed it. This war was at its height when the Yeats moved to Dublin.

The violence and bloodshed affected Yeats greatly and we see this concern in poetry he wrote during this time:

We had fed the heart on fantasies,
The heart's grown brutal from the fare;
More substance in our enmities
Than in our love.

THE SENATE

Yeats was invited by the new Irish government to take a seat in the Senate. He accepted gladly and took an active part in its debates and activities for the next six years. He showed courage in accepting the seat in the Senate because in 1922 those associated with the new government were in danger of being assassinated or having their houses burned down. Yeats now had to have an armed bodyguard. His house in Merrion Square had bullet holes in the windows and the bridge at Thoor Ballylee was blown up, filling the ground floor of the tower with water.

In 1923 Yeats's great talent was given world-wide recognition when he was awarded the Nobel Prize for literature. It was presented to him by the King of Sweden.

Back in Dublin he was busy writing, and managing the Abbey Theatre. In 1923 and 1924 plays by a new dramatist, Sean O'Casey, received an enthusiastic response from audiences. A new play by O'Casey, *The Plough and the Stars*, was presented in 1926. This time, however, many of the audience

Part of the crowd attending Yeats's funeral in Sligo.

were outraged by the play. They felt the play showed the Irish in a bad light and there were riots at each performance. On the fourth night, when the curtain had come down and there was pandemonium in the theatre, Yeats himself appeared on the stage. A silence descended on the audience at the sight of the great poet. Remembering the riots of twenty years earlier during Synge's plays, he addressed them with the words, 'You have disgraced your-selves again.' One of the actors said later, 'Yeats was like a lion that night, no one could have withstood him.'

Yeats was now in his sixties and his health was not very good. In 1928 his doctor suggested he should go abroad for a rest so he went to Italy with his wife and children. For the next few years he divided his time between Italy and Ireland. He spent the summer of 1931 at Coole Park with Lady Gregory who was very ill. On 22 May 1932 she died and Yeats was heartbroken to lose such an old and trusted friend.

Although he was in poor health himself, Yeats's life was still full of activity. He continued writing, maintained an interest in the running of the Abbey, gave lectures and travelled.

His home in Dublin was now a house called Riversdale in Rathfarnham. He was happy here with his wife and family. The house became the gathering point for friends from the old days and new younger writers. Among the friends who visited him here were Sean O'Casey, Frank O'Connor, Douglas Hyde and Maud Gonne. The happiness he drew from his friendships and family life at this time can be seen in his poetry. He wrote of himself at this time:

> All his happier dreams came true
> A small old house, wife, daughter, son,
> Grounds where plum and cabbage grew,
> Poets and Wits around him drew.

In the winter of 1938 Yeats and George went to stay in a hotel in the South of France. Here, on 28 January 1939, at the age of seventy-three, Yeats died.

The tombstone at Yeats's grave in Drumcliff, Sligo.

He had wanted to be buried in his beloved Sligo but the outbreak of the Second World War made this impossible and he was buried in France. When the war was over, Maud Gonne's son, Sean Mac-Bride, who was the Irish Minister for Foreign Affairs at the time, arranged for Yeats's body to be brought back to Ireland and buried in Drumcliff cemetery, Sligo, in accordance with the poet's wishes. An immense crowd attended the funeral, showing the high esteem in which the poet was held. A plain tombstone stands over his grave inscribed with the poet's own words.

PLACES TO GO AND THINGS TO SEE

5 Sandymount Avenue, Dublin — Yeats's birthplace

82 Merrion Square, Dublin — Yeats lived here

Riversdale, Rathfarnham, Dublin — Yeats's last Dublin home

Thoor Ballylee, Gort, Co. Galway — Yeats's tower and summer home

Coole Park, Gort, Co. Galway — Lady Gregory's home; the house is gone but the park is open

Autograph tree, Coole Park

Lissadell House, Co. Sligo — Home of the Gore-Booths

Drumcliffe Churchyard — Yeats is buried here and his headstone is engraved with his famous epitaph.

Glencar Waterfall, Co. Sligo

Ben Bulben, Rosses Point, Co. Sligo

National Gallery, Merrion Square, Dublin — Paintings by John Butler Yeats and Jack Yeats; also many portraits of Yeats, Maud Gonne and other friends, and many fellow writers and actors.

and

Municipal Gallery, Parnell Square, Dublin

Abbey Theatre, Abbey Street, Dublin — The present building is new. The old Abbey was burned down in 1951.

National Library of Ireland, Kildare Street, Dublin — Photographs and manuscripts.

DATE	YEATS	IRELAND	THE WORLD
1865	Born 13 June		American Civil War ends. Abraham Lincoln assassinated.
1867			Typewriter invented.
1870		Michael Davitt sentenced to 15 years penal servitude.	Charles Dickens's last book published.
1874	Yeats goes to Godolphin school, Hammersmith.		
1876			Battle Little Big Horn — Custer's 'last stand' — major American Indian victory.
1877		Davitt released. Parnell elected President of Home Rule movement.	
1879		Bad harvest. Land League founded with Parnell as leader.	Edison invents electric light.
1880	Yeats family return to Ireland.		
1881	Yeats goes to High School.	Davitt arrested. Parnell imprisoned. Land League banned.	
1882	Yeats writes first poems.	Phoenix Park murders.	
1883			R.L. Stevenson *Treasure Island* published.
1884	Yeats attends School of Art, Dublin.	GAA founded.	
1885	Yeats meets John O'Leary.		
1886		Defeat of Home Rule Bill. Land agitation begins again.	Marx *Das Kapital* published.

Year	Yeats	Ireland	World
1887	Yeats family return to England.		
1889	*The Wanderings of Oisin and Other Poems* published. Yeats meets Maud Gonne.		Eiffel Tower built in Paris — world's tallest structure at the time.
1891	Yeats and friends found the Rhymer's Club in London. Yeats founds Irish Literary Society. Proposes to Maud Gonne.	Death of Parnell.	
1892	Yeats founds Irish Literary Society in Dublin. *The Countess Cathleen* published.		
1893		Second Home Rule Bill defeated.	
1895			X rays discovered.
1896	Yeats moves to Woburn Buildings. Meets Lady Gregory. Meets J.M. Synge in Paris.		
1897			Queen Victoria's diamond jubilee — 50 years as queen. Height of power of British Empire.
1899	*The Countess Cathleen* performed in Dublin.		
1900		Home Rule parties reunite under John Redmond.	
1901			Death of Queen Victoria.

1903	Annie Horniman gives generously to help start Irish National Theatre. Maud Gonne marries Major MacBride. *In the Seven Wood* and other works published.		Wright Brothers first flight.
1904	The Abbey Theatre finds home in Abbey Street.		
1906			First general radio programme broadcast in U.S. Pablo Picasso and Braque develop cubism, a style of painting.
1907	Synge's *Playboy of the Western World* causes riots at Abbey. Yeats visits Italy.		
1908			First Model T Ford cars produced. Grahame *The Wind in the Willows* published.
1911		Anti-Home Rule campaign begins.	
1912			The Titanic sinks.
1913		Ulster Volunteers founded. Dublin lock-out strike. Irish Volunteers founded.	G.B. Shaw *Pygmalion* performed.
1914			Outbreak World War I.
1916	Writes poems on Rising.	Easter Rising.	
1917	Again proposes to Maud Gonne. Buys Thoor Ballylee. Marries George Hyde-Lees.	Sinn Féin wins by-elections.	Revolution in Russia.
1918			End World War I.

1919	Daughter Ann born. 'Wild Swans of Coole' written	Meeting of Dáil Eireann.
1921	Son Michael born.	Negotiations to end Anglo-Irish War. Treaty signed.
1922		Opening of North of Ireland Parliament. British withdraw from Ireland. Civil War begins.
1923	Yeats made Senator. Awarded Nobel Prize for literature.	Civil War ends.
1924		First Irish radio station. School attendance made compulsory.	First Labour Government in Britain. In Russia Lenin dies. Stalin takes over.
1926			General Strike in Britain.
1929			Wall Street Crash causes world economic depression.
1932	Lady Gregory dies.		
1922			Adolf Hitler comes to power in Germany.
1939	Yeats dies in France on 28 January.		Beginning World War II.
1948	Yeats's body returned to Ireland and buried at Drumcliff.